FLOWER PRESSING

by MARGE EATON   pictures by GEORGE OVERLIE

 Lerner Publications Company • Minneapolis, Minnesota

LIBRARY OF CONGRESS CATALOGING IN PUBLICATION DATA

Eaton, Marge.
  Flower pressing.

  (An Early Craft Book)
  SUMMARY: A how-to-do-it book explaining the technique
of pressing and preserving plants, flowers, and leaves, including
projects for independent learning.

  1. Pressed flower pictures—Juvenile literature. 2. Flowers—
Collection and preservation—Juvenile literature. [1. Pressed
flower pictures. 2. Flowers—Collection and preservation] I.
Overlie, George, illus. II. Title.

SB449.3.P7E2   745.92′8   72-13340
ISBN 0-8225-0855-9

Copyright © 1973 by Lerner Publications Company

ISBN No. 0-8225-0855-9
Library of Congress No. 72-13340
Printed in U.S.A.

Second Printing 1974

Contents

Meadow, forest, and marsh

A meadow on a sunny day is a treasure of sights, sounds, and smells. If you look closely, beneath the grasses and flowers, you will see ants scurrying in and out of their sand castles with food and news for their fellow citizens. You will also see caterpillars and spiders. They work for themselves. Bees and wasps hum pretty low notes that make the high, chirping bird songs sound sweeter.

And always, as the breezes puff and blow and kiss the creatures and plants on the living meadow, summer smells hover over the earth. The scent of clover, timothy, wild roses, and lush soil blend and freshen the air.

A century ago, much of our country was a meadow, a vast treasure. The people who lived on the meadow lands saved and used the treasures they found there. They gathered roots and herbs for teas and medicines. They followed the

orange hawkweed

bees to their hives and collected the honey. To brighten their lives during the cold winters, they also picked and dried the beautiful flowers and grasses.

You too can keep summer alive. You can learn how to press and dry flowers, grasses, and leaves. And you can learn how to make pretty pictures with them.

It is easy to find plants to press and dry. Different kinds of flowers grow in the meadows as the seasons change. There are buttercups in the spring. In mid-summer there are daisies and clover. In fall there are goldenrods and asters. And all summer long you can find many kinds of slender grasses in the fields.

The cool dark woods also have beautiful plants to gather and press. You can find pretty violets hidden under their green leaves. There are dainty ferns and leaves on the ground and in the trees.

You can also find interesting flowers in the marshy places. Irises are beautiful when they are pressed and dried. See if you can find a sundew. Touch the top of the sundew leaf very carefully. See how it closes up. The sundew is a plant that catches and "eats" tiny insects.

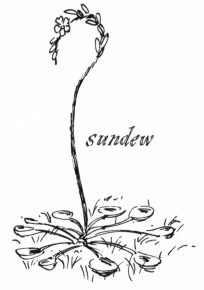

sundew

Wherever you live and wherever you travel, you can find flowers, leaves, and grasses to press and dry. It is easy to carry an old book along on a trip or a nature hike. As you gather the plants, you can carry them between the pages of the book.

Sightseeing is more fun if you look for new kinds of plant life. Wherever you pause on your walks, look for five different kinds of leaves and five different kinds of flowers. You are certain

lady's slipper

to find them. Scientists do not know for sure, but they believe that there are more than 350,000 varieties of plants on earth.

Flower petals and leaves should be as dry as possible when you pick them. Plants absorb moisture in the morning and evening, so the best time to collect is on dry, sunny afternoons.

You should also know that you are not allowed to pick some kinds of wild flowers. For example, in Minnesota, you cannot pick the state flower, the Lady's Slipper. Other states have different laws, and you should know them before you start collecting. You are also not allowed to pick flowers in state parks.

Collecting at home

A very good place to begin your collection is in your own yard. Pick some leaves from the bushes and trees. Do you have lilacs? Or a hedge with red berries? You can press the leaves from the hedge. You can press a flat cedar stem. Some leaves, like maple and oak leaves, have interesting shapes and will make pretty pictures by themselves. Other leaves, like mountain ash, grow on stems in groups of three or five. You might like to combine these leaves with flowers in a picture. It is better to press the whole group of leaves if they grow in groups.

Do you have flowers on your lawn? Look for clover, violets, or tiny grass flowers. Look in the vegetable garden too. Asparagus ferns, carrot tops, and pea vines have different shapes and colors. Be sure that the flowers and leaves you collect are perfect, with no spots or holes from insect bites.

If you live in an apartment, you can find grasses, leaves, and small flowers beside the sidewalks and on boulevards. Go to the park too, and you will see many kinds of plants that you might have overlooked before. And wherever you live, you can grow plants in pots inside the house.

A gallery of plants

These are a few of the many flowers, leaves, and grasses that press and dry nicely:

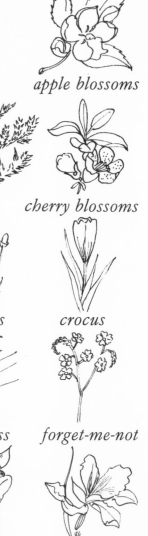

apple blossoms

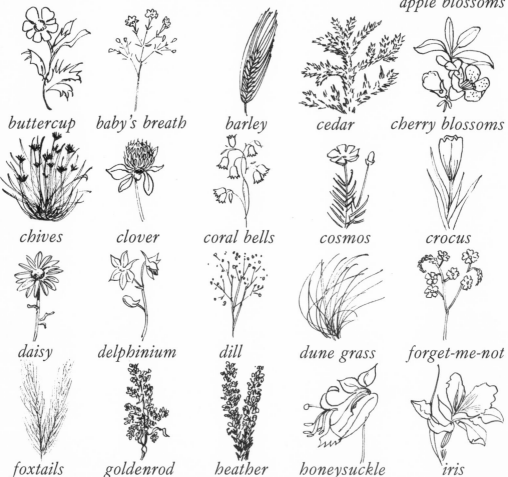

buttercup   *baby's breath*   *barley*   *cedar*   *cherry blossoms*

chives   *clover*   *coral bells*   *cosmos*   *crocus*

daisy   *delphinium*   *dill*   *dune grass*   *forget-me-not*

foxtails   *goldenrod*   *heather*   *honeysuckle*   *iris*

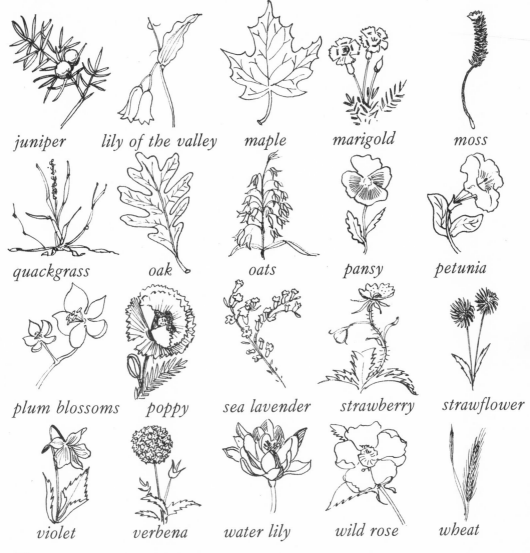

juniper   lily of the valley   maple   marigold   moss

quackgrass   oak   oats   pansy   petunia

plum blossoms   poppy   sea lavender   strawberry   strawflower

violet   verbena   water lily   wild rose   wheat

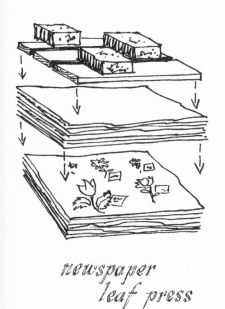

gathering book

*newspaper
leaf press*

How to press

For best results, you should press the plants as soon after picking as you can. If you are traveling, bring along several extra books. At the end of the day, put the flowers and leaves you have gathered in a book you are not using. You can press them when you get home.

When you are able to press your collection, you should set up the first press for leaves. Leaves are flat and easy to press. While you are working with leaves, keep the flowers you would like to press and dry between the pages of your collecting books.

To press leaves, first place them between heavy layers of newspaper. Put 12 sheets of newspaper on the bottom. Then arrange the leaves on the newspaper so that they do not touch each other. Put a label near each leaf so that you will be sure what kind it is when it has dried. Put 12 more sheets of newspaper on top of the leaves. Then put flat boards on top of the pile of newspapers. Finally, put two or three bricks on top of the boards to keep the leaves inside the newspapers flat.

12

Keep this press in a dry place for at least three weeks. It will be tempting, but do not peek at the leaves. If you do, you will cause them to wrinkle because they are not dry enough. After three weeks, the leaves will be dry and brittle, and you may take them out of the newspapers very carefully. While these leaves are drying, you may press some other plants.

When the leaves have been nicely settled in the board and newspaper press, you may press the flowers you have gathered. You may press them as you did the leaves, or you may use another kind of book press. But first you must prepare some of the flowers in a special way before you put them in a press because they are not always flat, and because they also fade or change color when they are dried.

When you begin to press flowers, you should choose at least some that are almost certain to keep their color and shape. Three flowers that keep their color and shape quite perfectly are pansies, daisies, and geraniums. Of course, you should experiment with the other kinds of flowers you have collected. Part of the fun of pressing flowers is finding out how different kinds of plants look when they are pressed.

Thick flowers and flowers that grow in groups need extra care. Geraniums are flowers that grow in groups. Geraniums press nicely if you cut each small group of flowers from the stem and press them separately. You should also cut the leaves from the stem, and then press and dry the leaves and stem. When you make your picture, you will put the geraniums back together again.

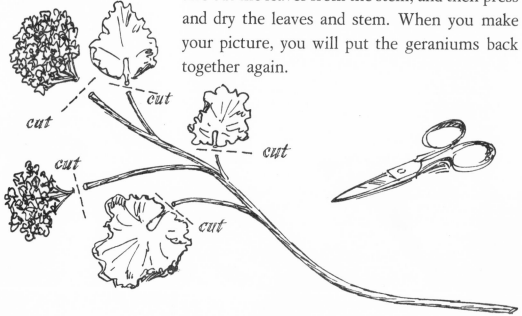

Daisies with large centers also require an extra step. To keep all parts of the daisy flat when it is drying, you must make a paper "pillow" for it. Lay the daisy on a thick piece of absorbent paper, like blotting paper. Then cut a hole that is the size of the center of the daisy from another piece of blotting paper. Put the paper with the hole in it over the center of the daisy. Cover the entire daisy with a third piece of blotting paper. When you press it, all parts of the flower will be under equal pressure.

Because you will be making a picture with the flowers and leaves you have collected, you will want to have some that stay very beautiful. But don't ignore the lowly weeds. They have a kind of beauty too, and they have interesting shapes and smells. When you make your picture, look for the beauty in all of the plants you have pressed.

You can use the board and newspaper press for very large flowers. But you can press and dry smaller flowers between the pages of an

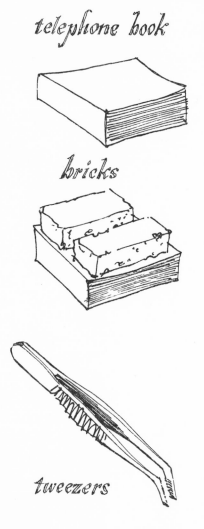

telephone book

bricks

tweezers

unused telephone book. The flowers should be placed face down on the page, and they should not touch one another. Label each flower. There ought to be at least 50 pages between flowers.

When all of the flowers have been neatly placed in the telephone book, place two bricks on top of it. Leave the telephone book in a dry place for four weeks. Again, do not peek at the flowers because they might wrinkle or break.

After four weeks, you may remove the dried flowers. Handle them with a tweezer because they will be very crisp and will break apart easily.

Store the pressed and dried flowers and leaves until you are ready to make your pictures. You may put them in a covered box. A shoe box is excellent for storing dried plants. Put a layer of paper between each flower in the box. This will also protect them from breaking.

Don't be surprised if the pressed and dried flowers change color. Some flowers become lighter or darker or lose their color entirely.

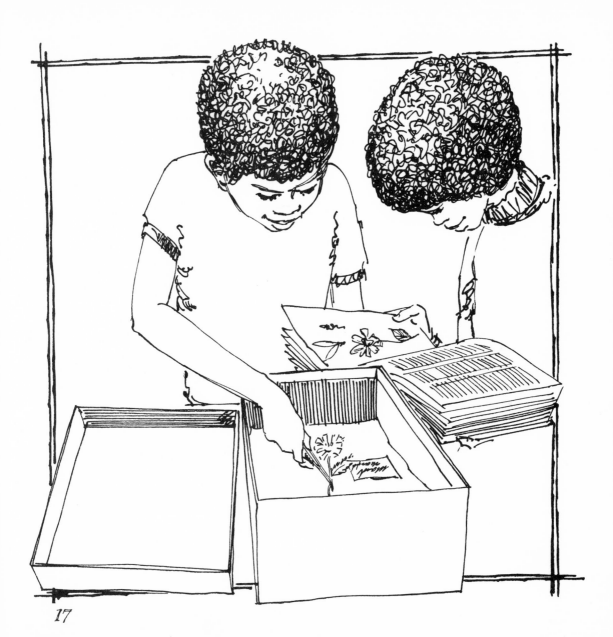

Restoring color

White flowers will often turn brown or purple. Pink flowers may change to brown, white, or purple. A bright purple may turn black, but a light purple will stay the same color. You might have the best luck with yellow and orange flowers when you begin. They do not change. A bright red color is not easy to keep. A red flower may turn dull and brown if it is not put in a press soon after it is picked. If too much color is lost when the flower is dried, you may carefully paint the faded petals with watercolors. If the paint runs off the petals, add a few drops of liquid detergent to the paint. Your flowers will look bright and alive again.

Making a picture

When you have many pretty flowers and leaves in storage boxes, you are ready to begin to make your first picture. Your picture will be covered with glass and held together by a frame so that the pressed flowers and leaves do not break or crumble.

dime store frame

used frame

Dime stores have nice frames that do not cost much. You will want one that is easy to take apart and put together again. Perhaps you have a frame at home that you can use. You might have a picture that you no longer hang on your wall. The frame from that picture can be used for your new hobby.

After you have found a frame, you must select a background for your picture. The background may be made of cloth or paper. Choose a color for the background that you think will match and blend with the flowers and leaves you have selected. Many people like plain black or white backgrounds.

If you choose a paper background, you should know that some colored papers fade with time. The construction paper you use in school is made in many pretty colors, but these colors often fade. Brighter colors fade more quickly than pale colors. Nice writing paper makes a good background.

You may choose a cloth background. If you

want to make your picture with dainty flowers and leaves, a soft cloth like velvet is nice. For more sturdy flowers and leaves, you might want to try a stiff cloth like burlap.

When you have decided on the kind of background you would like to have for your picture, you must cut it to fit the frame. Cut it so that it is the same size as the cardboard that slips into the back of the frame.

Now you are ready to design your picture. Try different designs on a separate sheet of paper. Lay the leaves and grasses down first. Then arrange the flowers between and among them. This is a time when you will really learn to appreciate the shapes and textures of common plants and weeds.

Then add some large flowers. The colors of the flowers should match and blend with each other and the background. Fill in the design with smaller flowers. Try different designs, but don't try to put all of your flowers in the first picture. Make the design simple.

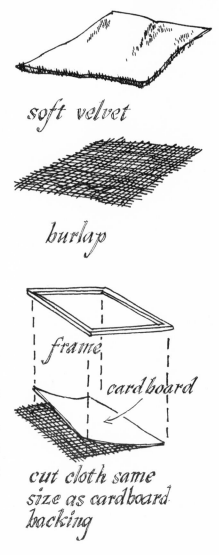

soft velvet

burlap

frame

cardboard

cut cloth same size as cardboard backing

Planning
a design

paper the
size of cloth

When you are happy with your design, you may begin the last part of your project—gluing the leaves and flowers into place. If you have chosen a cloth background, you must glue it to the cardboard back of the picture frame before you attach the dried plants. Use only a very few dots of glue on the cloth, and let it dry thoroughly.

Then move your design to the background and glue the flowers and leaves to it. It is very important that you use only a little glue, so begin by putting a small dot of white glue on a piece of waxed paper or aluminum foil. Dip a toothpick into the glue and touch it to the back of the flowers and leaves. Then place them on the background. Do not let the flowers and leaves get wet with too much glue, and handle them carefully with a tweezer so that they do not break. Don't sneeze, or your pretty design could blow right off the table!

Let your picture dry completely and slip it carefully into the frame. You can hang the

waxed paper

drop of glue

picture anywhere. Perhaps you would like to save a large spot on a wall in your room for more pressed flower pictures. Make other pictures with larger and smaller frames and hang them around your first picture. You can keep many summer memories on that wall.

Other projects

Would you like to make a serving tray for parties or treats with your friends? You can make one from the metal lid of a large container. Or you can buy an inexpensive metal tray from the dime store. You will need glass or Plexiglas to cover the pressed flowers after they have been glued down, so you must also get a piece from the hardware store cut to fit the top of the tray. Plexiglas is clear, flexible plastic and it is easy to handle. If you choose Plexiglas, you must smooth the edges with fine sandpaper before you use it. Sand carefully so that you do not scratch the top or bottom of the Plexiglas.

To make the tray, you must again choose a background for the flower design. Use heavy

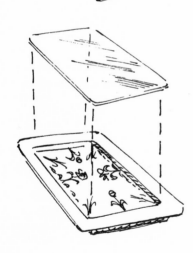

paper or a stiff fabric such as burlap or canvas. Cut the background to fit the bottom of the tray. Glue it down and let it dry as you did with the picture. Then arrange the pressed flowers and leaves on top of the background. This time, you might like to arrange the flowers so that the design "makes sense" from any angle. Perhaps you could place the flowers in a circle around the edge of the tray. Put one perfect round flower in the center. Then glue the flowers down and let them dry.

You will also use glue to fasten the glass or Plexiglas surface to the tray. Apply a line of glue all around the bottom of the inside edge of the tray. Set the surface glass into the tray. The glue will hold it firmly in place.

You can make many of the things in your room and your house more beautiful with pressed flowers. They can be glued onto any wood, paper, or cloth surface.

You might like to decorate a wastebasket with flowers or grasses. Measure the height and the distance around the middle of the basket. Then cut out a rectangle of burlap or canvas that is that wide and that long. Arrange a pleasing assortment of pressed plants on the burlap and glue them down. Glue the fabric to the wastebasket and let it dry. Then spray the fabric and flowers with acrylic lacquer. You can get acrylic lacquer at a hobby shop.

measure height and distance around

mark and cut

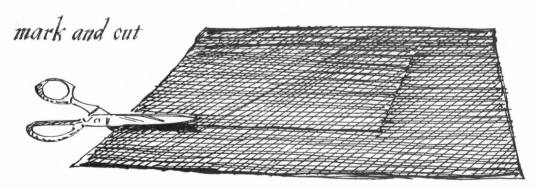

Decorated Waste basket

Card Designs

Acrylic lacquer can be used to protect pressed flowers on many different objects. You can make greeting cards and place cards with pressed flowers and fine stationery. Fold the card or paper. Glue the flowers onto the front of it, and, if you are making a place card, write your guest's name on the card as well. Spray the flowers and the front of the card or paper with lacquer.

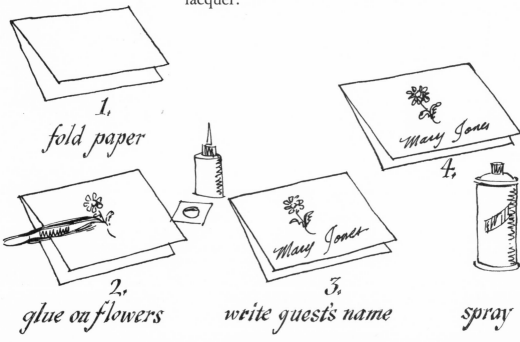

1.
fold paper

2.
glue on flowers

3.
write guest's name

4.

spray

28

You can decorate holiday candles. Use thick candles that burn slowly. Glue flowers around the base of the candle and spray them with lacquer. Make Easter decorations too. Blow out some eggs and dye them if you wish. Then glue flowers onto them and spray. Add some gold braid, and you can hang the eggs on the Christmas tree.

Holiday Candles

Easter decorations

Christmas decorations

29

Even the smell of summer and spice can be kept until Christmas. Let's make a *potpourri* (PO-poor-ee) like our great-great grandmothers did. During the summer you should go on a special flower hunt. Gather the most fragrant flowers you can find. Lilies of the valley, roses, lilacs, and honeysuckle can be found in your yard or in the meadow. You can buy carnations or gardenias. They smell very sweet. Remove the petals from the body of the flower and dry them on paper towels or newspaper in a warm place for about a week. When they are dry, sprinkle the petals with salt. Then mix these spices together: one teaspoon of cloves, one teaspoon of cinnamon, one teaspoon of allspice, one teaspoon of nutmeg. Buy one ounce of orris root from the drugstore, and get one ounce of brown sugar from your kitchen. Then find a pretty jar with a wide mouth and a tight top.

Put the potpourri together in layers like this:

Grandmother's potpourri

← repeat layers

← spice mixture
← brown sugar
← orris root
← petals

Repeat the layers until you have used all of the ingredients.

Let the mixture age. Shake it about once a week. When a month has passed, you can open the jar whenever you want to freshen your room or smell a good smell.

31

In learning to collect, save, and use the bounty of the meadows and forests, you will learn more about our precious natural world and its treasures. There is not much of this world left, and we cannot let it slip away from us. It is our standard of order and beauty.